# LIVING WITH A NARCISSIST

## JANELL BROWN

**Living With A Narcissist**

**Copyright** © 2020 Janell Brown

All rights reserved.

***Living With A Narcissist*, by Janell Brown.** No part of this book may be reproduced in any written, electronic, recording, or photocopying form without written permission of the author, Janell Brown.

Books may be purchased in quantity and/or special sales by contacting the publisher, Janell Brown, by email at JanellTeach@yahoo.com.

Editing:
Tanisha Stewart at tanishastewart.author@gmail.com

Indie Ink at indieink.net

Cover Design:

Tyora Moody at tywebbincreations.com

First Edition
Published in the United States of America
by Janell Brown

## CONTENTS

| | |
|---|---:|
| Chapter 1 | 1 |
| Chapter 2 | 7 |
| Chapter 3 | 11 |
| Chapter 4 | 19 |
| Chapter 5 | 25 |
| Chapter 6 | 31 |
| Chapter 7 | 35 |
| Chapter 8 | 41 |
| Chapter 9 | 47 |
| Chapter 10 | 55 |
| Chapter 11 | 61 |
| Chapter 12 | 67 |
| Chapter 13 | 71 |
| Chapter 14 | 75 |
| Chapter 15 | 79 |
| Chapter 16 | 83 |
| Chapter 17 | 87 |
| Chapter 18 | 91 |
| Chapter 19 | 93 |
| Chapter 20 | 95 |

# Chapter ONE

It was early July. Summer was just beginning.

Life was going great. A single Black woman loving Jesus.

Things were perfect until I met him. That was when my life was turned upside down.

Sometimes you have to be careful what you wish for. Or should I say, be careful what you pray for.

Come with me as I take you through the journey.

Here's how it all began.

It was six in the morning and my son woke me up out of my dream.

I was disappointed because my dream was so perfect. I actually met the love of my life.

I had to get up and get going, though, because today was my son's birthday and there was a lot we had to do to prepare for the party.

My two besties, Tamra and Ja'el, were helping me to prepare.

In just a few hours the party would begin.

While cooking, I revealed my dream to my friends.

They hung onto my every word as I was telling them.

Right when I got to the best part I was interrupted by a phone call.

"Hello?" I answered.

"Hello, may I speak to Lexis?" the woman on the other end asked.

"Speaking. How may I help you?"

"Lexis, hi! I'm Amy. I'm from the Generation of Christ National Church choir."

My heart thumped in my chest. "Hi, Amy. Glad to hear from you!"

"Thank you. I have a question for you, Lexis. We are looking for a soloist to come and be a part of our studio album project. We have heard you sing many times and love your beautiful voice. We believe that it would flow perfectly with our choir. Would you be interested in sharing your gift on our album for the Glory of God?"

I almost said yes before she finished speaking, but I withheld my excitement.

After she finished her last sentence I said, "Amy, that sounds like a beautiful idea. How do we get started?"

I listened as Amy gave me the details. I grabbed my pen and notepad that were attached to my refrigerator by magnets.

When I hung up the phone my jaw dropped.

"They want me!" I announced.

Ja'el and Tamra swept me up in a group hug.

We were so excited that we almost forgot about the food that was cooking.

I wiped happy tears from my eyes.

"Thank you, Lord!" I raised my hands to Jesus because I knew He was the only one who could have caused this situation to work out in my favor.

"Amen, praise Him!" said Tamra.

"Wow, Lexis," Ja'el said. "Everything is finally coming together for you."

My heart was swelling with joy, but those words from Ja'el's mouth put a slight damper on my spirit. "Well, Ja'el, not everything."

Both of my friends looked at me with concern.

"I'm still waiting on my husband." *Lord, when are you going to send him?*

I focused on the pot of spaghetti I was making.

Around seven in the evening the party was going great.

My besties stayed with me when all of the children left and helped me clean up.

After I put my son to bed I wrapped my hair, and I couldn't help but think about my dream.

My fantasy man was so strong, tall, and handsome.

I wondered if I would ever meet a man like that in real life.

*Could this be a sign?*

*I hope so.*

When I finished wrapping my hair I went to my prayer room and began to pray.

I poured my heart out to God about my dream.

After a while, my eyelids became heavy, so I went to my bedroom to sleep.

―――

The next day my son was not back home from school yet, so I headed to the grocery store to get the ingredients to prepare one of his favorite meals which was veggie lasagna.

I figured we had the spaghetti yesterday, so why not make today a pasta day, too?

As I was reaching for the sauce I noticed a strong, tall, handsome man standing next to me.

He graciously reached for the sauce for me.

"Did you need a little help with that?" He smiled and

his teeth were so white I could practically see my reflection in them.

*Oh, my...*

I put my head down because I was so shy and nervous suddenly.

At the same time, I was in awe of how handsome he was.

From the look in his eyes he seemed to feel the same way about me.

He handed me the sauce. "If I can, may I ask you your name?"

"Lexis. What is yours?" I fought to hold back the huge smile that was growing on my face just from talking to this man.

"I'm Tyson." There were those perfect teeth again. "I just moved to the state and I'm settling in the area." He eyed my grocery basket. "Hm. You preparing a nice meal for someone?"

"Yes," I blushed. "I'm preparing for my son."

I said it that way to drop the hint that I was single.

The conversation continued for a few more moments and it seemed that Tyson and I had some chemistry between us.

I looked at his bare ring finger.

"Are you married?"

It was Tyson's turn to blush. "No, Ma'am. I'm not. I'm actually looking for a beautiful and God-fearing woman to settle down with."

*Kind of like me.* I chuckled, feeling a bit more confident.

"Well, I happen to be a woman of God who is also looking for a godly man."

I thought to myself, *Could this possibly be the one?*

He smiled again. "Can I have your number? I would love to get to know you further, Miss Woman of God."

I gave it to him.

Later that evening he texted me.

**Mr. Tyson:** *Miss Lexis, would you mind accompanying me to dinner this Friday?*

My smile was as wide as the room now that he wasn't in front of me watching.

My fingers flew across my phone's keyboard.

**Me:** *Absolutely, Mr. Tyson.*

I was so excited I had to call my girls up and let them know what happened.

That Friday, Tyson and I went on our dinner date.

I was extremely excited, but I downplayed it so he wouldn't know.

I didn't want to give him the impression that I was desperately looking for someone.

As the night wore on and we ate our dinner, we had a wonderful time.

We laughed and joked, talked about our love for the Lord and church, and the more we interacted, the deeper I fell for him.

I felt like I knew him. Like we were connected.

We stared into each other's eyes and shared our dreams and goals for the future.

Before we knew it the restaurant was closing.

"Whew!" Tyson remarked when we were making our way to his car. "Who knew time would fly by so quickly?"

I watched as he clicked his key fob to unlock his doors, then he opened the passenger side door for me and took my hand to assist me inside.

I was so impressed by this man.

He bought me flowers at the beginning of the date,

held an intelligent, charming, spirit-filled, and genuine conversation throughout, and my hand hadn't touched the bill or any door since I'd been in his presence.

He felt like a Godsend.

*I can't wait to see where this goes.*

# Chapter Two

Tyson and I were chatting on the phone on my way to work.

I loved to hear his deep baritone voice over my Bluetooth.

It was so peaceful and soothing.

"Tyson, I remember you mentioning that you were looking for a church home. I was wondering if you would be interested in visiting my church?"

I felt a little nervous to hear his response, but he agreed.

"You know, Lexis, I feel like you read my mind. That is a great idea. I'd love to join you."

My heart leapt with excitement as I took this as another sign of confirmation from the Lord that this man was a keeper.

I still didn't want to get too far ahead in my thinking, but Tyson certainly had promise.

That Sunday was yet another confirmation.

Tyson showed up before I did, and when I walked up to the front door, he held it open for us.

During the service Tyson sang along with the songs, shouted during the praise break, and raised his hands to the Lord during worship.

He even shouted *amen* as the pastor preached.

He was clearly a devoted man of God.

His Bible was well worn, and the pages were wrinkled like he spent much time devoted in study and prayer.

One of the mothers turned to me when Tyson wasn't looking and winked, signaling her approval.

*Okay now, Lord. Are you trying to tell me something?*

When we exited the building Tyson had to wipe sweat from his brow because he had been praising so hard during the final praise break. It was impromptu and had occurred as the pastor brought the message to a close.

"Lexis, that was remarkable!" He looked at me in amazement. "You have such a wellspring of knowledge and greatness here at this church. No wonder you are such a sweet and beautiful woman of God."

I blushed. "Thank you, Tyson. I'm glad you enjoyed it. Please feel free to come back and visit us any time."

Tyson's expression turned serious suddenly. "Now that you mentioned that, Lexis, I felt a pull in my heart during the pastor's sermon. I'm going to pray about it tonight, but I believe God may have called me to join this congregation."

I lit up like a Christmas tree. "Oh, Tyson, that is wonderful! So glad to hear it!"

"Are you going to Bible study on Wednesday?" he asked, studying the program that the usher had given him at the beginning of the service. "I would love to accompany you if I'm not being too forward." He looked nervous now. "I'm sorry, I don't mean to intrude."

I quickly reassured him. "Absolutely not! I would love for you to join us at Bible study."

I was in awe of this man.

More and more he was showing me that he was exactly what I was looking for.

I almost burst into tears at that thought.

God was truly answering my prayers.

As we were walking down the steps of the church toward Tyson's car, my besties Ja'el and Tamra waved from where they were standing in the parking lot.

I brought Tyson over to introduce him.

"Ja'el, Tamra, this is Tyson."

"Nice to meet you," Tamra smiled.

Ja'el extended her hand as well. "Hello, Tyson."

They exchanged small talk for a moment and then it was time for us to go.

Later on that evening, we had a three-way call to debrief about Tyson.

"So, ladies... what did you think?"

I studied their facial expressions through my phone as I spoke. We were on a video call.

Tamra spoke first. "Lexis, I'm excited for you. Tyson is so handsome, and he seems so godly and so nice."

"I agree," said Ja'el, "But Lexis, remember to take your time. You may like this man, but everyone is not always who they appear to be at first."

Ja'el was the realist of our trio, as she called herself. Tamra was the optimist, and I was somewhere in the middle.

"Of course, I will, Ja'el. I'm not desperate. I want a husband, but I want a man of God as well."

*And Tyson appears to be just that.*

"That's right. You want a man of God, not a wolf in sheep's clothing."

Now I was offended, but I didn't show it.

"Yes, we do have to make sure that we are not dealing with someone who is untruthful, but Tyson is not that. He opens doors, he buys me flowers, he texts me morning affirmations, and he wants to come to Bible study this

Wednesday. I have never met a man that actually asked me to go to Bible study instead of the other way around. All these good things cannot be ignored. Plus, I can tell he reads his Bible just by looking at it."

Ja'el studied me as I spoke. "Lexis, I am very happy for you. I am just reminding you to take your time, that's all."

I calmed down.

Maybe I misunderstood her intentions.

"Sorry if I sounded like I was worked up. I agree with you, Ja'el. I will take my time."

Tamra smiled. "Keep us updated."

I didn't like the way Tamra just said that.

*What does she mean, 'keep us updated?' Who says I have to answer to them? I just told them about all the wonderful things Tyson has done, and they are trying to ruin my moment? Not today.*

"Listen ladies, I have to go. I have to get up early tomorrow morning."

# Chapter THREE

Tyson and I had been going steady for a few months now and I was liking him more and more. He was such a good man to me.

We just finished yet another beautiful date.

The night was still young, so we decided to take a walk down the street by one of the cities' largest bridges. It had a beautiful view of the stars and the water underneath us glistened in the moonlight.

It was so romantic.

Tyson's large and muscular hand felt so strong and protective as it held mine.

Our fingers were woven together like a perfect symmetry.

Tyson stopped short for a moment and looked at me.

"What is it?" I stared up into his deep brown eyes.

"Lexis, I've been trying to hold back my feelings for a month now, but I can't do it any longer."

My breath caught in my throat. "What do you mean?"

He choked up. "Everything about you. You're so beautiful, so sweet, so gentle and loving. I feel nurtured with the love of God when I'm with you. You are exactly what I am looking for in a woman."

My heart was beating rapidly in my chest.

"Lexis, what I am trying to say is I feel a way for you that I have never felt for another woman before. I love you. I'm falling in love with you."

I was taken aback by this news.

"Oh, Tyson!" My eyes filled with tears as I realized this was a dream come true. "I feel the same way about you. I'm falling in love with you, too!"

Tyson broke out in a wide smile. "See, woman... it's past ten in the evening and I know you have to wake early for work and so do I, for that matter. Can we possibly go out Friday night to celebrate our confession of love?"

*Celebrate our confession of love... where did the Lord find this man?*

Then my face fell.

"What's wrong?" Tyson's brows furrowed.

"I almost forgot, Tyson. Friday is my family night with my son. I promised we would stay up and play video games together."

He nodded in understanding. "Oh... I understand."

"Well, how about Saturday? I'll be free then and I can have my mom watch him."

His smile returned. "Sounds like a plan!"

―――――

Friday was going to be epic as my son called it.

We laid out all of his favorite games, and even some new ones he begged me for at the mall, but I didn't mind spoiling him a little. He was a very good boy.

He did well in school and all his teachers loved him.

I never had a problem out of him, so I tried to give him as much of what he wanted as I could being a single mother.

As my son and I were in the middle of a playful banter about which game we would play first, and who would win, the doorbell rang.

"Who is that?" I asked. "I didn't order the pizza yet."

I opened the door and my jaw dropped when I saw Tyson.

He was holding some video games and puzzles in one hand, and pizza and soda in the other.

I grabbed the soda before it could roll off the top of the pizza box where Tyson had it balancing.

"Tyson, what are you doing here?"

I felt a little funny about him showing up, especially since I told him this was family night with me and my son.

Tyson and I hadn't had the conversation about him meeting my son yet, but here he was at the door.

I was very protective about Fridays.

I wanted my child and I to have a bond like no other.

Tyson assessed my expression and must have noticed I was a little apprehensive.

"Oh, please don't take offense. I didn't mean anything by it. I just know how important Fridays are for you, as you explained, and I wanted to join in the fun."

I thought about it for a moment, then I reasoned that it wouldn't hurt for Tyson to join us for one night.

Besides, my son was friendly anyway, so he probably wouldn't mind.

I let him in and the games began.

By the end of the night my heart was full of happiness.

At first, I was upset about Tyson showing up, but when I saw how he and my son got along so perfectly I thought, *maybe this is what God wants. Maybe this is how He ordained it to be.*

---

The next night was my singing engagement at Generation of Christ.

I was excited, yet nervous, because not only was I going to be able to use my gift of singing to glorify God on a live recording for the choir's album, but also a very famous gospel music producer, Clive Odell, was supposed to be there and I heard he was looking for new artists!

It was beyond my wildest dreams to even sing in front of Mr. Odell, but to know that he was looking for artists, and that I could potentially have an opportunity to work with him?

God was truly moving in my life.

"Lord, please use my voice tonight and please help me make a good impression for Mr. Odell. I'm not sure if he is really looking for artists like they say he is, but if he is, Lord have your way."

God truly was a present help because as soon as I stepped out onto the stage in front of the choir all of my fears disappeared as God's anointing took over.

At the end of the song the spirit of worship was so strong in the room that you could cut it with a butter knife.

Then, all of a sudden the drums sounded and praise broke through the atmosphere.

"Glory!" I shouted into the microphone as the Holy Spirit spoke over me. "The Lord is in this place! Praise Him! Praise Him, everybody!"

Everyone was up and out their seats, including some people in the choir stands.

In the midst of the beautiful moment, I even saw Mr. Odell raising his hands and shouting unto God.

The pastor that was hosting the event approached me after it was over.

His voice was hoarse from the thunderous mini sermon he did during one of the choir's other songs.

"Ms. Lexis, you brought down the house, young lady. God has truly gifted you."

I blushed at those words, reverting back to my shy, reserved self. "Thank you so much, Pastor. I enjoyed your message during the song."

"Glory to God. You know that wasn't even planned?"

My eyes widened. "It wasn't?"

He shook his head. "Nope, but that's how God works sometimes."

"Amen. He knows who needs what and when."

"That's a word," the pastor said, and he walked away to get some of the free refreshments they were serving in the lobby of the building.

I felt someone's eyes on me and noticed that Tyson was sitting in the back of the church.

I had no idea that he was there and I didn't even know that he knew about the event.

I brushed it off, however, because he might have seen a flyer or something.

Besides, who was I to say he couldn't come?

He made his way toward me just as Mr. Odell stopped as he was passing by.

"Lexis? Am I remembering your name correctly?" he asked.

My heart thumped. "Yes, Sir. That's me!"

His eyes widened. "My God... young lady, you have a voice on you. God has truly gifted you. Are you currently signed with any production companies?"

*Is he really asking?*

*Is this really happening?*
*Oh my God. Yes, Lord!*

"No, Sir. I am not signed with anyone at the moment."

He smiled and pulled a card out of his pocket. "Well, Lexis, I would be honored to offer you an opportunity to work with our company. We would start you off by having you do a few engagements, contracted, of course. If that works out we will talk about even greater opportunities."

I could not believe my dreams were coming true right before my eyes.

Tyson had made his way to where we were standing by now.

He clapped his hands. "This is so great! God is blessing you, Lexis!" he turned to Mr. Odell. "Of course, she would love the opportunity."

Mr. Odell studied Tyson for a moment then turned his attention to me.

"So, I take that as a yes?" There was a question in his eyes, probably because he wanted to hear it from my mouth.

I thought it was kind of rude for Tyson to jump in like that, but I didn't say anything.

"Yes, Sir. I'd be honored," I said to Mr. Odell.

I took his card, and we scheduled an appointment to speak about the first singing engagement with his company in a few weeks.

When Mr. Odell walked away Tyson covered his mouth. "You know what, Lexis, my apologies. I shouldn't have cut into your conversation like that."

My expression softened because that was exactly what I was about to say to him.

"It's fine," I reassured him. "You were just trying to help."

He let out a deep breath. "Whew! So glad you aren't upset."

The more I thought about it, the more I became amazed by Tyson's charm.

He was so thoughtful and helpful... God had truly blessed me with this man.

# Chapter Four

Time was really flying. I felt like Tyson and I were like two peas in a pod.

We'd been spending so much time together that I hadn't seen Tamra and Ja'el in weeks.

I guess that was what people meant when they said when a woman meets a good man she suddenly forgets her friends.

Of course, I hadn't forgotten about my girls.

They had been with me through thick and thin.

I purposed in my heart to give them a call so we could catch up with each other soon.

I wondered if either of them had come across a man as good as Tyson yet.

Tyson and I had just went on yet another perfect date, and this one was for the books. We watched a romantic comedy at the movies, and it was so funny our sides were hurting from all of that laughing.

"Whew," Tyson wiped his eyes. "That was so good we might have to come back and see it again."

"Agreed," I said, and waited for him to open the passenger side door.

He did, and held his hand out as usual to assist me as I got in.

*Such a sweetheart,* I mused.

We chatted on the way to my house, then when we

pulled up, Tyson walked around to the passenger side to open the door for me so I could get out.

When I was unclicking my seatbelt to get out Tyson held his hand up to stop me.

"What?" I let the belt slide back to its position after it was unclicked, but I remained in my seat looking at Tyson.

My eyes widened as I watched Tyson get down on his knee.

"Tyson, what are you doing?"

I was stunned as Tyson pulled out a small ring box from Tiffany's.

*How did he know? I was just looking up rings from that place the other day!*

He looked up at me with a smile.

"Lexis, in just a few short months you have stolen my heart. I cried out to God for a woman that would understand me. A woman that was gentle and loving and kind. A Godly woman, and He gave me all of that and much, much more when He gave me you."

I opened my mouth to respond, but Tyson halted my words and made my jaw drop when he belted out the first few lines of the famous song *You Are So Beautiful* by Joe Crocker.

I was absolutely floored as my eyes filled with tears. I didn't even know Tyson could sing!

After he finished the last line, he wiped the single tear that had rolled down his cheek, then he continued his speech.

"Lexis, my love, my beauty. I want to wake up to you every morning and go to sleep with you every night. I want you to be the mother of my future children as we build an even bigger family with you and your son. All this, of course, if you will have me. Will you marry me?"

I had heard of proposals before, but Tyson deserved some kind of award for this.

"Yes!" I practically yelled it at the top of my lungs, but I didn't care. The world needed to know that I loved this man, and that he loved me.

Tyson slipped the ring on my finger. It was beautiful. He helped me to my feet and I threw my arms around his neck. He wrapped his around my waist.

We shared a long, passionate, and soulful kiss.

When we finished, Tyson was so excited he picked me up and twirled me around.

Later on, I went into my prayer room and thanked God for my soon to be husband. "Thank you, Lord. Things are finally coming together for me."

---

I finally caught up with Ja'el and Tamra via video chat to tell them about the engagement.

"... and then he picked me up and twirled me around! It was magical." My eyes watered as I gushed out the ending of the story.

Tamra looked like she was about to cry, too. "Oh, Lexis! I am so happy for you. I know how long you have been waiting for this."

Ja'el, however, looked leery.

"Listen, Lexis... Don't take this the wrong way, but I honestly think it's too soon."

My heart dropped.

My mind was immediately brought back to the first time we discussed Tyson and how Ja'el seemed to have nothing but negative things to say about him even then.

"Ja'el, let me ask you something." My eyes narrowed as I spoke.

She cocked her head. "Yes?"

"Are you jealous of my relationship with Tyson?"

Her jaw dropped. "Jealous? You think I'm jealous?"

"That's what it sounds like."

Tamra tried to cut in because Ja'el and I had butted heads before so she probably thought we would go there today.

"Lexis, I don't think she meant it that way."

"Sounds like it to me."

Ja'el spoke up. "Listen Lexis, I'm not trying to hate on you. I'm just concerned about you as a friend. I'm sure you would feel the same about me if you saw what I am seeing."

My eyes narrowed. "And what exactly do you think you are seeing?"

Yes, I had an attitude, and no I didn't care.

How was she going to react this way as my best friend when I told her I was getting engaged? Where was her excitement? Where were the congratulations?

Instead of her understanding where I was coming from as a single woman who had finally found the love of her life she found nothing but negative things to say about my happiness.

I was not trying to hear it today.

"Listen, I have to go."

Tamra protested. "Lexis, wait."

Too late. I hung up the phone and ignored their calls when they tried to reach out to me again.

The next day, Ja'el texted me: *Listen, Lexis. I thought about our conversation last night, and I'm sorry. I should have celebrated your moment with you rather than bring up anything negative. I hope you accept my apology and know that I am here to support you every step of the way.*

I smiled when I read that, and quickly texted her back. *No problem. Thank you. I appreciate you always looking out for me.*

---

When I got to work, I could hardly contain my excitement.

I wrestled back and forth about whether I should tell everyone about my ring, or whether I should just let them notice it.

I decided on the latter because I didn't want to bring too much attention to myself.

The day started off normally, with no one noticing my ring because I stayed in my office.

About a half hour before my lunch break, my boss knocked, then walked in carrying some papers. "Lexis, could you–"

She halted her words mid-sentence.

I looked up at her and saw that she was staring at my ring.

Her face broke out into a huge, but curious smile.

"What is that?" she drawled.

I normally kept my private life private, but I decided to spill the beans this one time.

"I got engaged."

Her hand cupped her mouth. "Oh, Lexis I'm so happy for you! Congratulations!"

She set the papers on my desk and walked around to where I was sitting to give me a hug.

We chatted for a few moments, then she told me what

she originally came in the office for, which was to create some new reports that were due at the end of the week.

By the time she left, I was already back into my routine.

A few more moments passed and a few more of my coworkers knocked and asked to come in.

I let them and they all oohed and awed over my ring.

I was excited and embarrassed at the same time.

It felt great to know that so many people were rooting for me.

# Chapter Five

After what felt like forever, my wedding day was finally here.

Tyson and I dressed in all white, and every one of our family and friends attended our celebration of love.

Once the ceremony was over, it was time to head to the reception.

The lights were soft, the food was fragrant, and the music was perfectly selected.

We had a combination of old school R&B, gospel, and jazz playing in the background.

It was such a peaceful atmosphere.

I watched from the head table as Tyson's mother and my mother seemed to be having a good conversation. Tyson's mother made a joke, and my mother cocked her head back and laughed.

"Thank God," I breathed. I was so glad that this day was going off without a hitch.

I looked over at Ja'el and Tamra.

They seemed to be heavily engrossed in a good conversation with some of Tyson's male cousins.

"Mm hm," I smirked. Ja'el made all of those remarks before, but it looked like she was attracted to Melvin from the way that she was staring at him as he spoke.

I made a note to tease her about it later.

Tyson finished his sparkling apple cider and gently grabbed my elbow.

"May I have this dance?" He smiled.

I nodded. "Yes, you may."

He whisked me onto the dance floor, and before we knew it, everyone joined in the fun.

By the end of the night, Tyson and I were so exhausted, but we were eager to get to our hotel room so we could end our first night as husband and wife properly.

We exited the venue hand in hand and waved at everyone to say goodbye.

The crowd was all smiles as the limo driver opened the door for us.

"We really did it, Lexus!" Tyson was grinning from ear to ear.

His excitement was contagious, so I found myself grinning as well.

"That we did. I can't believe I am finally your wife."

He kissed my hand. "To today, and many more beautiful days like this."

"Amen."

———

I woke up the next morning a very happy woman.

I was so refreshed after getting a good night's sleep, although Tyson and I didn't actually close our eyes until a few hours ago.

We had our own party in the bedroom after we got to the hotel suite.

It was so romantic.

Tyson and I seemed to be compatible in every way.

I loved my husband.

"Thank you, Lord..." I breathed with a smile, and then I turned and saw that Tyson wasn't in the bed next to me.

I looked at the alarm clock next to my side of the bed.

"Where could he be?" I asked, seeing that it was only nine in the morning.

Tyson said he didn't have much money, so I ended up footing the bill for most of our festivities for this weekend.

I paid for the hotel room on my credit card, and I also had the food catered at our reception.

Tyson and his family covered the fee for renting the church, but that was only two hundred dollars.

When I asked him to go half on my wedding dress at least, he told me that he had an emergency bill that came up, so I just brushed it off.

He couldn't help with any of the festivities for our honeymoon weekend, either, which surprised me, but I wasn't going to complain.

I was committed to being a good and supportive wife.

We were in this together.

But now Tyson was out somewhere.

"Calm down, Lexis. Don't be so uptight. He has the rest of his life to make it up to you, and he started last night."

I smiled again as I remembered how passionate Tyson was.

God had truly blessed me with this man.

Tyson entered the room a few minutes later.

"Where were you?" I wrinkled my nose.

"Oh, I checked out the gym downstairs. It's state of the art!" That was when I noticed he was sweaty.

I relaxed.

"Shower?" he smirked, noticing that I was still in the bed.

"Sure," I smirked back, and we took our first of what I hoped to be many romantic showers together.

After that, we went downstairs to enjoy a nice continental breakfast, courtesy of the package we ordered from the hotel.

---

Tyson and I are adjusting to our life as newlyweds, and things are going well.

We seemed to work perfectly in sync.

Tyson got along with my son, our work schedules were balanced, and that caused me to feel at peace.

I had heard horror stories about stepparent and stepchild relationships, as well as husbands and wives barely having time for each other due to being too busy.

Everything was perfect.

I was on my way to work when I got a text from Tyson asking me to cook his favorite meal tonight.

It was the third time this week, and we had planned to alternate cooking, but I thought nothing of it.

I texted him back. *Sure! I'll pick up some groceries on the way home.*

He replied immediately. *Thank you, Beautiful.*

I blushed.

*You're welcome, Handsome.*

*Oh, I forgot to mention: I'll be working a little late tonight.*

I frowned. *Okay. See you when you get in.*

I was actually hoping that we could eat out tonight since I had been so stressed at work,

but I didn't mind preparing a meal for my husband since he loved my cooking.

When I got off work, I picked up the groceries as promised.

I cooked the meal listening to one of my favorite gospel playlists as I worked.

Just as me and my son were sitting down to eat, Tyson walked in the door.

I looked at the time on the stove, then at him. "Oh, I thought you were working late today?"

He paused like he was confused, then his expression relaxed.

"Oh, my boss ended up letting me go early."

I didn't say anything because the food was already done.

Tyson sat down and relaxed with me and my son.

# Chapter Six

Some time had gone by, and I noticed that some things changed.

I felt like I was a housewife doing nothing but cooking and cleaning.

I thought Tyson and I were going to work as a team, like we discussed before we got married, but things didn't seem to be working out that way.

I felt like I was getting more and more tired every day.

I hadn't been to the salon in ages.

My hair needed some serious work.

I looked at my nails. Most of them were missing polish, and the ones that did have some left had cracks in them.

I made a mental note to get my hair and nails done as soon as I could.

This Friday would be the perfect day.

Later on that evening, Tyson stormed into the house startling me and my son as we played video games.

I assessed my husband's features, noticing that he was clearly upset.

"What's wrong, Tyson? What is it?"

Tyson paced back and forth. "My boss fired me."

I was shocked. "What happened?"

He paused. "It was over some nonsense."

"What kind of nonsense?"

Now my son was interested, too. He looked up at

Tyson as we awaited his response, the video game long forgotten.

Tyson shrugged it off. "Don't worry about it."

I didn't press it right then because I didn't want to cause an argument in front of my son. Tyson seemed to be a little testy.

Later on that night, I asked him again. "What happened with your job, Tyson?"

He tensed. "I'm feeling really overwhelmed right now, Lexis. Just give me some time to cool down."

I wanted to press it, but decided not to.

"Tomorrow morning I'll be up bright and early looking for another job."

That made me feel better, although I was still put off by the fact that he didn't want to communicate with me.

Still, I reasoned that being a peaceful wife was the best way, so I let it go.

---

A few weeks went by, and Tyson still didn't have another job.

All of the bills were on my back.

"Tyson, if you aren't able to find something quickly, it's fine. I have some savings that we can use. I set it aside in case we needed it for a rainy day."

Tyson seemed relieved.

"Thank you so much. I actually needed to borrow a few dollars. I promise to pay you back."

I hesitated, because when I said it was a rainy-day fund, I meant that it was supposed to be used for bills and household expenses, but I agreed.

"Okay Tyson, I'll give you some, but just to reiterate,

this is a rainy-day fund. This is the only savings I have, so I want to make sure that we don't run through it."

"I understand completely. I will replace the money. Thank you so much, babe."

Later that day, I was sweeping in the kitchen and I went to change the trash.

Tyson was out at the library filling out applications for a new job, so I decided to get some things done around the house.

As I was changing it, the bag snagged on the corner of the counter and all of the trash fell out onto the floor.

"Oh no!" I went to get a fresh bag to replace the one I had accidentally ripped.

I put some gloves on and bent down to pick up all the big items to throw them in the new bag.

As I was putting the trash into the new bag, I noticed an opened envelope that said *Final Paycheck*.

"What is this?" I wrinkled my nose.

I opened it out of curiosity and noticed two strange things.

Number one, the date of Tyson's last paycheck was dated weeks before he had stormed in that night saying he got fired.

Number two, the paycheck was docked three hundred dollars.

My eyes widened when I saw that. "Why would they dock his paycheck and why would he lie and tell me he just lost his job when it seems like he's been out of work for quite some time?"

I was confused and upset all at once.

———

Once my son was in bed, Tyson and I got into our first real argument.

"When did you really get fired, Tyson?" I held the envelope out for him to see. "What really happened?"

He didn't answer my questions.

Instead, he tried to redirect.

"Lexis, I'm so sorry. I would never mean to upset you. I did get fired a few weeks before I told you, but I was trying to hurry and find another job before you found out. I was ashamed. I'm your husband. No man ever wants to say this to his wife."

I stared at him. "Why did they dock your pay?"

His eyes shifted. "Oh, that was a clerical error. They overpaid me on one of my previous checks, then remembered to take it out on the final one."

Something told me that Tyson was not being truthful with his responses, but I decided to let it go.

At least he was being honest now about losing the job.

*Maybe it really was a clerical error.*

I decided to try not to be too suspicious.

# Chapter SEVEN

I looked at myself in the mirror.

Dark circles were starting to appear under my eyes and I was beginning to gain a little weight due to eating a lot of comfort food.

Tyson finally found another job, but since it was so strenuous, as he described it, he didn't have the strength to help me around the house.

I was forced to do it all by myself.

I thought to myself, *You know what? I am the wife. Let me just try to be a good wife.*

I worked a full-time job, then I had to come home, cook, clean, and help my son with his homework.

Tyson was too tired to contribute.

It became hard on my body.

I felt myself getting so tired.

As I gained a few more pounds, Tyson seemed to notice. "Hey, you've been putting on a few pounds there, Lexis."

I took my eyes off the pint of ice cream I was eating out of.

I had only taken a few bites, but now I felt my appetite decreasing.

"I've just been so tired lately, Tyson."

"Well maybe you should take some time and go to the gym."

I had to remind him that I didn't have time for the

gym. "I have so many responsibilities to take care of. Working, cooking, cleaning..."

He looked like he wasn't hearing me.

"Master Fitness is open twenty-four hours. Why don't you get a membership?"

I stared at him. "Well, can you pick up on some things around the house so I can have more energy to go?"

"Sounds like a deal."

But several more weeks passed, and Tyson never lifted a finger.

One thing that did seem to be going well for me was my budding music career.

I recorded my first single and was set to do a mini tour of various churches in the area soon.

My first performance was coming up in a few nights.

I was so excited for the opportunity.

That was one thing to be proud of.

---

Tonight was the night.

I was going to be on stage, pouring my heart out to the Lord, and I could not wait.

I rushed home because I needed every spare moment to get ready.

I picked the perfect colors and style for the evening to really brand myself well as an up and coming gospel artist.

Tyson promised to pick up my dress, so all I had to do was come home, shower, fix my hair, and do my make up.

My heart pounded with every step.

When I walked in, I immediately noticed something was off.

Tyson was lounging on the couch, still in his sweatpants.

"Where's the dress?" I asked.

"What dress?" He looked confused.

"The dress for tonight!" I felt my blood pressure rising.

"Oh, I forgot all about your event."

I fumed, forcing my tears back. "Can you go pick up the dress, Tyson? I can't be late. I have to get in the shower and get myself together."

Tyson didn't seem to notice that I was stressed out. "I got you."

He got up with a nonchalant attitude, took his time, and strode out the door.

I raced through the house trying to get ready.

I showered and put my makeup on in record time.

I stood in my slip and bathrobe at the bottom of the stairs, waiting for Tyson to hurry up and walk in the door with my dress.

After ten more minutes, I called him.

"Tyson, where are you?"

"I'm at a drive thru. I had to stop to get something to eat since you won't be home."

I felt myself getting frustrated.

I burst into tears. "Tyson, you are acting like you don't even care. I thought tonight was just as important for you as it was for me. This could be our ticket to get out of this place and move to Hollywood. This could be our ticket to make it big. You act as if you don't even care."

He hung up on me.

Another ten minutes passed and Tyson finally walked in the door with the dress.

He handed it to me and walked away.

He didn't make any effort himself to get ready so he could come along and support me.

Instead, he plopped right back down on the sofa.

When I raced back down the stairs after putting my dress on, he finally spoke.

"I feel like you are neglecting your duties around the house."

I didn't even respond.

I just went to my performance.

Despite the fact that I showed up late, Mr. Odell said he was still considering signing me.

He looked at me over his glasses.

"Will you be able to come on the two-week tour? Just to try it out?"

"Absolutely!" I gushed, temporarily forgetting all about Tyson.

When I got back home, Tyson wasn't there.

I called him and he didn't answer, so I texted him: *Where are you?*

Fifteen minutes later, he texted back: *I was called into work. Hope the event went well.*

I was upset that he picked up hours instead of supporting me, but I let it go, reasoning that he probably needed the money.

———

The next morning, Tyson still wasn't home, so I couldn't share the good news with him.

He texted me a few hours after I woke up, claiming he was working a double.

I felt like there was something wrong with that, since he never worked a double before, but I shrugged it off.

I went to work, came home, cooked, and cleaned.

Tyson finally came home.

I disregarded the fact that he was way too late to have only worked a double and came right out with my good news.

"I was asked to go on a tour! Mr. Odell is thinking of signing me!"

Tyson didn't look the least bit excited.

He shrugged. "That's good."

My son was sitting in the living room playing video games, and I knew he could hear our exchange, so I didn't confront Tyson about his attitude.

Later on that night, I couldn't take it anymore.

"What was up with your response earlier?" I asked.

He looked at me. "What response?"

"To my potential record deal, and the fact that I am going on tour."

He ignored my statement, dropping another bomb instead.

"My boss laid me off."

I froze.

"I thought you just worked a double?"

"I did. She laid me off when I was done."

This was too much for me to take in.

I was just about to ask him what was really going on with him when he continued.

"So, since I lost my job you can't take off work to go on tour."

"But we need the money!"

I felt like my dreams were vanishing right in front of me.

"This is a lifetime opportunity, Tyson!"

He still had his nonchalant attitude.

He shrugged. "I want my wife at home. I need your support. I need you home with me."

I was crushed. I didn't know what to say.

As we got into bed, I cried and begged him to let me go on the tour.

He said no.

I told him that this was my dream and what I had been wanting to do since I was a little girl.

I felt like this was my calling.

He ignored me and turned over.

I cried harder, but he acted like he couldn't hear me.

Soon, he was snoring.

I was pouring my eyes out right beside him, but my husband was fast asleep.

## Chapter EIGHT

When I told Mr. Odell that I could not make it to the tour, he told me that it was fine. He had another singer he could use.

But it wasn't fine.

I was crushed.

I couldn't believe I really had to deny my lifetime dream.

"Lord, it hurts so bad," I cried on my way home from the meeting.

At that moment, I got a call from Ja'el on my Bluetooth.

I didn't really feel like talking, but I hadn't spoken to her or Tamra in a while, so I picked up.

"Hello?" I made sure my voice didn't betray my emotions.

"Hey, Mrs. Celebrity! I heard you are going on tour soon!" Ja'el sounded excited for me.

"Can we come?" Tamra joked.

I guess they had me on three way.

It would have been a great moment of celebration between the three of us, but I had to ruin it with the bad news.

"I'm not going, guys. I just left the meeting with Mr. Odell."

"What?" they said in unison.

"What happened, Lexis?" Tamra asked.

"I had to give it up. We need the money from my job, so I can't take the time off of work."

"And how does Tyson feel about this?" Ja'el asked.

I heard the hint in her tone, but I wasn't going down that road with her today.

I was wondering more and more every day exactly what kind of man Tyson really was, but I wouldn't dare say that to my friends.

Ja'el would probably have field day with that information because she told me I was moving too fast when I said we were getting married in the first place.

I kept my mouth shut.

―――

When I got home, Tyson was sitting on the couch once again.

He was dressed in his sweatpants and a t-shirt.

"Hey, did you forget about the Bible study tonight?" I asked.

I was leading worship, and Tyson and I were supposed to go together.

He didn't budge.

"I'm not going."

"Why not?"

He kept his eyes on the TV screen as he spoke. "Church is not the answer to everything."

I went upstairs to get ready, mulling over Tyson's words the whole time.

When I came back downstairs to leave, he was sitting in the same spot.

He hadn't moved an inch.

I went to the Bible study, led the worship, and learned a lot from the pastor's teaching.

But I couldn't get Tyson out of my mind.

*What did he mean the church is not the answer for everything? What is he saying?*

A scripture came to my mind about encouraging oneself: 1 Samuel 30:6.

When I got back to my car after church, I turned my phone back on and saw a missed call and a text from Tyson.

*Playing pool with the guys. I'll see you later tonight.*

I found myself getting frustrated.

Tyson had missed Bible study for the second time, and now he was going to play pool with his friends?

My life was becoming so lonely and empty, despite the fact that I was married.

I felt like a single woman.

---

As time wore on, Tyson missed more and more Bible studies and church gatherings.

I was wondering why he suddenly no longer seemed to be interested in church, so I decided to ask him one day.

His response shocked me, to say the least.

"I'm my own pastor. I don't need anybody telling me what the Bible says. I can read it for myself. Besides, all those pastors want is your money, anyway."

I had no idea where this was coming from because Tyson claimed to be a Christian when we first met.

Now, all of a sudden, he was his own pastor and had an entirely different set of beliefs.

I figured it might just be a phase, so later on that night

I tried to gain a connection with him. I was longing for intimacy.

I sat down and tried to talk to him.

Before I could finish my sentence Tyson held his hand up.

"Please, Lexis. I'm not in the mood to have any discussions. I want to be left alone right now."

I was hurt, but I brushed it off the best that I could.

The next day, I was headed to work and Tyson was sitting on the couch watching TV.

An idea came to mind.

"Hey, Tyson. Would you mind cleaning up a little while I'm at work since you will be home? It would help me out a lot. I'm so tired at the end of the evening."

Tyson looked at me like I was crazy.

"I ain't doing no woman's work. That's what's wrong with you women these days. Don't know how to keep a man happy."

I paused. "What do you mean by that?"

"Nothing. Actually, I was looking into getting us a housekeeper."

I blinked. "What? A housekeeper?"

Tyson nodded. "Yes, to help around the house so you won't be so stressed and so tired all the time."

"No, thank you. I would rather handle the household duties myself. Or you can just help out."

Tyson sneered. "Are you sure you can handle it? You seem like the type of woman who can't have too many things on your plate."

I felt myself growing hot. "And what do you mean by that?"

"Look at you," he gestured. "You're gaining weight. Your hair is never done. Your nails are chipping, and you haven't bought an outfit in ages. You're slipping. You're letting yourself go."

I couldn't believe my ears.

Before I could open my mouth to respond, Tyson continued.

"Those kinds of things make a man develop a wandering eye."

I was at a loss for words.

"You know what a wandering eye is, don't you?"

"Does that mean you're cheating on me?"

He calmed down.

"No, I didn't say that. I was just speaking hypothetically."

"Well, that was a heck of a hypothetical scenario."

He shrugged. "Like I said, it was hypothetical. Weren't you heading to work?"

He didn't even kiss me goodbye or wish me a good day.

I rushed out the door and went to work, trying to focus on my responsibilities for the day.

I couldn't believe the way my husband had spoken to me.

## Chapter NINE

Tyson finally found another job.

He'd been there for a few months, which was good, but unfortunately things have not changed at home.

When he gets home he rushes off to go out with "friends".

We barely spent time together.

I felt like a broken record with all the times I begged for him to spend time with me. "Do you even want to be married anymore?" I asked. "It's like we are nothing more than roommates!"

He sighed. "Okay, Lexis. You'll get your wish. Let's go to Mad Matties."

I wrinkled my nose. "Mad Matties? Isn't that a bar?"

He nodded. "Yes, it is. It's a calming atmosphere."

"Tyson, you know I'm a minister and a worship leader. I don't go to bars."

"Well, do you want to spend time together or not?"

I thought about it.

Desperate to connect with my husband, I agreed.

---

We went to the bar.

I put on a nice blouse and some loose-fitting jeans with some pumps to top off my outfit.

Tyson was wearing a muscle shirt and some slacks.

It seemed like as soon as we got there Tyson was throwing back shot after shot.

I had been sipping on the same glass of wine the whole time we were there.

The more time wore on, the less I saw the point in this outing for me and Tyson.

I tried to spark conversation with my husband, but it seemed like he was more interested in the bottoms of his shot glasses than he was in me.

I even tried to crack a few jokes, but he only gave me polite chuckles as his eyes shifted in the direction of other women.

Finally, I was fed up.

"I have to go to the bathroom," I announced as I stood.

Tyson looked like he barely heard what I said.

There was a woman in a halter top and short skirt that was walking by, and Tyson was preoccupied with staring at her.

As I was making my way to the bathroom a thought came to mind.

*Let me see what kind of man Tyson really is.*

There was a waitress walking by. I pulled her to the side.

"I want you to do me a favor," I said. "When I go to the restroom I want you to write a random phone number on a sheet of paper and give it to my husband sitting over there." I gestured toward Tyson.

She nodded.

"I just want to see if he will take it, knowing that I'm with him. When I come back I want you to tell me if he took the number or not."

She agreed. "Absolutely, Ma'am. I'll get right to it."
"Thank you." I shook her hand.

When I returned from the restroom I looked at the waitress.

She nodded, indicating that Tyson took the number.

I was furious.

At that point I was ready to go home.

Tyson threw back another shot as I approached him.

I faced him with a grim expression.

"Hey. I'm ready to go."

He stood.

"Cool. I'll drive."

"No, you've been drinking."

"I know how to drive, Lexis."

His eyes narrowed.

I didn't think it was a good idea at all, but I didn't want to argue with him in front of all of these people, so I agreed.

As I buckled my seatbelt, I prayed that we wouldn't get into an accident.

Tyson began driving and we ended up on the highway.

I remained silent.

Tyson finally noticed.

"What's wrong with you?"

His breath smelled like the alcohol he had consumed at the bar.

I turned away from him in disgust.

"Nothing."

*This man is nowhere near who I thought he was.*

"Lexus, talk to me."

I couldn't believe him. The whole night, I was trying to get his attention, and now he wants to talk? On our way home? After he accepted another woman's number?

I couldn't help myself.

"I know you took that number from the lady at the bar!"

Tyson paused.

"Lexis, I don't know what you're talking about."

"Don't play with me, Tyson. That woman told me herself what you did. How do you think that makes me feel as your wife? I was sitting right across from you the whole night and as soon as I step away for a moment, you take another woman's number?"

Tyson kept his eyes on the road. "Lexis, calm down. It wasn't that serious."

"Not that serious?! Wow."

My mind was blown.

He tried to save face. "I was never going to call the number. I was going to throw it away as soon as we got to the house."

I wanted so bad to open my mouth and say, "Throw it away, huh? Would that be before or after you saved it to your contacts in your phone?"

But I didn't.

I remained silent to try to calm myself, but my feelings were getting the best of me.

"Tyson, I think I might want a divorce."

He was silent for a moment, then he turned to me with a wild look in his eyes.

"You will never leave me!"

"Yes, I will!"

He increased the speed in response.

"Tyson, slow down."

He ignored me, going even faster.

"Tyson!"

His expression was stony.

"Say you're not leaving me, Lexis. I will kill both of us."

I became afraid.

"Tyson, please."

"No. Say it."

He increased the speed more, and now we were going over eighty miles an hour.

"TYSON!"

He was driving like a madman, weaving through the traffic and barely missing other cars.

We got so close to some of the bumpers I almost had a heart attack.

Tyson looked like he was having an out of body experience.

Like his mind was no longer there, and his body was in full control.

I called the police.

"Hello, hello! I need help!"

The operator tried to calm me down.

"Where are you, Ma'am?"

I gave her the name of the highway. "My husband is driving over one hundred miles per hour, and he will not slow down. Please send someone."

"What exit are you near?"

As soon as the operator said those words, Tyson slowed down to a normal rate of speed.

My heart rate decreased.

"I think he's calm now."

"Are you sure?"

"Yes, Ma'am."

"Well call us back if there are any further issues."

"I will."

When I hung up, Tyson drove in silence for a few

moments, then he roughly turned off the side of the road and parked in a wooded area.

"Tyson, what are you doing?"

He removed the keys from the ignition and got out of the car before disappearing into the woods.

The night was becoming more and more bizarre by the moment.

I locked the car and followed him.

"Tyson? Tyson!"

He kept going deeper and deeper into the woods, repeatedly saying something to himself.

I couldn't make out what he was saying.

After about ten minutes of walking, he stopped short.

"Tyson, what is going on?"

His voice cracked as he spoke.

"I don't want to lose you, Lexis. Can we please just try counseling? Please."

"Tyson, I'm willing to try it, but can we please just go home? We're in the middle of the woods, and it's not safe out here. Our car is abandoned back there."

Tyson agreed, and we made our way back to the car.

Since he had the keys, he drove, and I didn't protest this time.

He drove in silence.

On our way home, I kept thinking over and over, *There is no way out. This man wants to kill me!*

―――

The day came for our counseling appointment.

I was eager to get started.

Pastor Morgan came highly recommended as a Christian practitioner, so I was grateful for this opportunity. His office was one of the best in the area.

The session started off well with us exchanging pleasantries.

Things went left, however, when it seemed that Pastor Morgan was taking my side.

Tyson acted as if he could not see any areas where he had gone wrong.

His main goal during this session seemed to be to point out all of my flaws.

Pastor Morgan wasn't having it, however.

He looked Tyson right in his eyes.

"Tyson, I understand you have some concerns, but I really don't think you are hearing your wife's side of these issues."

Tyson was furious at that. He stood.

"This is outrageous!"

I could see the veins popping out of his neck.

"You are trying to come on to my wife. I will not stand for this."

Pastor Morgan looked confused. "Tyson, I'm not trying to approach your wife."

Tyson turned to me. "Come on. Let's go, Lexis."

I looked from Pastor Morgan to Tyson, full of embarrassment.

Tyson stormed out of the office, not bothering to wait for me as he walked down the hallway.

"My apologies, Pastor Morgan," I said.

He nodded. "It's fine, Lexis. I've seen worse. Take care of yourself."

I rushed out the door and to the parking lot where Tyson was already sitting in the driver's seat.

He started in on me as soon as I got in the car.

"I've seen enough, Lexis. I will not have another man disrespect me right to my face."

"Tyson, I don't think he was-"

He held his hand up.

"I don't need any counseling, Lexis. I'm going to make changes on my own. I see the areas that need improvement, and I vow this day to renew my commitment to you and see to it that we move past this hurdle."

I sat back in my seat as Tyson pulled out of the parking lot.

Tyson's tone was so full of conviction, I believed what he said.

# Chapter TEN

Tyson and I went to a family dinner at Tyson's sister's house.

This is the first of our attempts to rekindle our relationship.

I figured it wouldn't hurt to give it another chance.

We hadn't been married that long, anyway.

Everyone said the first few years are always the hardest.

The dinner went okay at first, but as the night wore on, I began to notice more and more that there appeared to be a big secret between Tyson and his family, and the secret was about me. Everybody was looking at me funny.

Tyson had also completely changed his personality.

He was acting like a golden child and his family was soaking it up. They seemed to fall for his behavior, but he acted nothing like that at home.

I wasn't sure what to make of it.

I wondered more and more what the big secret was, then his sister shot Tyson a glance and asked me, "So, Lexis, how are you enjoying your marriage?"

From the look on her face, and the rest of his families' expressions, I knew Tyson had been talking about me behind my back.

I immediately felt outnumbered.

Only God knew what he had told them.

When we got home I decided to confront the issue head on.

"Tyson, why did your family ask about our marriage?"

He shrugged. "They just want to see how we're doing. I haven't told them anything."

I didn't believe him, but of course I didn't have proof either, so I just decided to leave it alone.

---

The next morning when I woke up, Tyson was still sleeping, so I jumped in the shower to get ready for church.

When I returned to the bedroom, he wasn't in there anymore.

I heard the TV downstairs in the living room.

I finished putting on my outfit and applied my makeup before spraying my perfume.

I grabbed my purse and was ready to head out the door.

When I got downstairs, Tyson was standing in front of the door.

"What are you doing?" I asked.

He stared at me. "You're not going."

"What do you mean?"

He repeated himself. "You're not going to church."

"Get out of the way, Tyson."

He refused to move.

"You said you wanted to work on the marriage. Here's your chance. I want to be with my wife intimately. Right now."

"Tyson, I am about to go to church. You heard me in the bathroom. You know it's Sunday."

"But I am your husband."

"Tyson, stop playing. You know I have to be there. I have to worship."

"You said you wanted to connect with me. This is how I want to do it."

I felt myself getting frustrated.

"Why couldn't we do this last night?"

"I was tired."

"Tyson, I'm already dressed. I didn't even get a chance to tell them I couldn't make it. Nobody is even there to stand in for me."

"I don't care. Get undressed. This is our marriage."

I opened my mouth to protest again, but he cut me off.

"Lexis, I'm trying to be faithful to you, but you have to meet my needs."

It felt like a catch twenty-two.

I didn't know what to do.

I ended up giving in to Tyson's demands and having sex with him instead of going to church.

When Wednesday came, he tried the same thing before Bible study.

I stopped him.

"No, Tyson. This will not become a pattern."

On my way out the door, he hurled his next words at me.

"If you keep neglecting my needs, you can't turn around and get mad if I look in another direction."

That almost stopped me in my tracks, but another side of me was not going to give in.

I went to Bible study, but the whole time I was there I thought about Tyson and his threats.

I began to seriously consider leaving again.

*But how do I leave? See how he reacted last time.*

That was my biggest concern.

I realized the only way to do it was to develop a plan.

A plan that Tyson could know nothing about.

---

Later that evening, I had a dinner date with Ja'el and Tamra.

We talked about life, but I kept my conversation short and to the point.

I didn't want to reveal too many details about my situation with Tyson.

I already knew how they felt.

I didn't know what to do.

"Oh," Ja'el said, her eyes lighting up like she was remembering something. "Lexis, I meant to tell you. I saw Tyson the other day coming out of Longhorn Steakhouse."

I tried to play it cool.

"Oh really?"

She nodded. "Yes, it was around one o'clock on Wednesday. I tried to wave to him, but he didn't see me."

Tyson's lunch breaks were set at his job. He only had a half hour, and they were scheduled at eleven.

That could only mean one thing, but I remained solid.

When I got home, I was ready to confront Tyson.

"Tyson, why were you at Longhorn Steakhouse at one o'clock on Wednesday? Ja'el said she saw you leaving."

Tyson looked tongue tied for a second, then he caught his stride.

"I don't know what Ja'el is talking about. My lunch break is at eleven."

My eyes narrowed. "She said she saw you, Tyson."

"Well, your friend is crazy. She doesn't know what she

saw. She didn't see me anywhere. I was at work, like I told you."

That was when I noticed the passion mark on his neck.

"Ja'el is crazy, huh? Well what is that on your neck?"

I pointed.

He played like he had no idea what I meant.

"What is what?"

I sighed. "Look in the mirror, Tyson."

He strode to the mirror in the living room, then turned back to me.

"You did that."

"No, I didn't! I'm not a teenager, Tyson, so tell me what is going on!"

It was time to put my foot down.

Tyson turned up the heat as well.

"Lexis, you did it."

"Just admit you have another woman!"

"I would never admit that because I'm not cheating. I'm telling you, you did it. You may not remember it, but you did."

I pressed him further, but I was starting to question myself since he was so adamant.

Then, he changed directions.

"Oh, you know what? Let me look again."

He did.

"This is actually a bug bite."

I didn't know what to think after that.

*Am I going crazy, or is he just a really good liar?*

Tyson seemed thoroughly convinced that everything he was saying was true.

# Chapter Eleven

I returned home from work one day to see Tyson's car parked outside, meaning he was home early.

There was another car parked on the street across from our apartment, which was strange.

I parked behind Tyson's car and looked over at the other car.

There were two women inside. They looked upset when they saw me and drove off.

When I walked into the house, I caught Tyson peeking through the blinds, but he straightened up when I saw him.

"Who were they?" I asked.

"Who were who?" He played dumb.

"The two women, Tyson."

"What two women?"

"The two women outside. The ones you were just watching through the blinds!"

"I didn't see any women. I don't know what you're talking about. I was looking to see if that was you pulling up."

I opened my mouth to speak, but gave up.

I was not going in circles with Tyson today.

I went to the kitchen and cooked, and Tyson, my son and I ate a silent dinner.

―――

The next morning, I woke up to see that three of my tires were flat and my windshield was bashed in.

I had no idea how all that happened without my alarm sounding off.

I was furious.

"Tyson, come look at my car!" I fumed from the front door.

Tyson ran down the stairs from our bedroom, looking guilty.

He walked around my car, seeing the tires and windshield.

"Oh wow." He glanced at his car, which was perfectly intact. "Did you take pictures?"

My eyes were filled with tears. "No, I didn't take pictures, Tyson! I called you."

"Let me order you an Uber, so you can get to work."

"Why can't you give me a ride?"

He came up with an excuse. "I have an appointment I need to get to, and I can't be late. Otherwise, you know I would have brought you. I'm sorry."

I didn't even bother to respond to that.

I waited for the Uber and got to work a few minutes late.

As I was walking in, it dawned on me that the two women from last night probably had something to do with my car being vandalized.

I was going to have to talk to Tyson about it when I got home.

My emotions got the best of me, and before I knew it I was crying.

My boss was walking by my office as I sniffled.

"Lexis, are you okay?"

I straightened up and grabbed a Kleenex.

"I'm fine."

"Are you sure?" She studied my features. "Do you want to take the rest of the day off?"

"No, I'm okay. Thank you for asking."

*I would end up just having to take an Uber anyway.*

When I got off work, I waited outside for the Uber that Tyson was supposed to order for me, but it never came.

My husband really left me stranded at work.

I whipped out my phone to call him.

I was tired and frustrated. I just wanted to get home.

"Hello?" he answered on the fifth ring.

"Tyson, where is the Uber you were supposed to order for me?"

"Oh... I forgot. I was on the phone with your insurance company. Unfortunately, we have some bad news, Lexis."

I tensed.

"What kind of bad news?"

I thought today could not get any worse.

"They said that since only three tires were flat, they aren't going to cover it."

I sucked my teeth. "Are you serious?"

"Don't get an attitude with me."

He hung up.

I could not believe that man.

Just then, I remembered that tonight was Bible study.

I ordered my own Uber and went to church. As soon as I got there, one of the deacons approached me. "Sister Lexis, would you mind leading praise and worship tonight? The person that was supposed to do it called in sick."

I felt overwhelmed with my own situations and

certainly didn't feel like I had the strength to lead others to worship, but I agreed.

"Of course."

He smiled. "Thank you so much, Sister."

Then he walked away.

I put all of my feelings aside, breathed a silent prayer, and walked to the front of the church.

"Lord, take over..." I prayed again before I picked up the microphone.

God answered my prayer.

The worship was mighty and the power of the Holy Spirit could be felt throughout the room.

Although my worship was sincere, my heart was crying out.

I was hoping someone would catch a glimpse of my pain and suffering, but no one did.

The entire congregation was on their feet, hands raised and mouths open, praising God and shouting, but I could barely lift my head.

I began to cry.

I tried to make my tears look like they were due to the spirit of worship that was in the room, but I was really weeping over the fact that my marriage was falling apart.

"That was so beautiful, Sister," the deacon smiled as I passed him on my way out. "We always know we can count on you."

I wanted to burst into tears all over again, but I held it back.

---

When I got home, the drama continued.

As soon as I walked in the door, Tyson was on my back.

"Where were you?" he demanded.

I was starting to develop a headache. "I was at church, Tyson."

His eyes looked like they were about to pop from their sockets. "At church? How dare you!"

"How dare I?" I was puzzled by his contempt.

"How dare you go to church after work when you know you were supposed to come home!"

"Tyson, I called you to ask about the Uber you were supposed to order for me, but you hung up on me, remember? Were you going to help me pay for that?"

I only asked that question to see what he would say.

"I'm not paying for anything since you only went to church to be petty."

I was fed up. It was time to let Tyson know how I really felt.

The words tumbled out of my mouth.

"Tyson, I want to separate. This marriage is becoming too much for me."

He got a wild look in his eyes. The same look he had when he was driving that night we were coming home from the bar. He approached me.

I stepped back as he moved forward.

Once I was against the wall and had nowhere to go he stood there, imposing his height on me for a few moments, then he walked away.

"Tyson! Please, if you don't change I will leave."

He continued to walk away without answering me.

He remained silent for the rest of the night.

My mind felt like it was going crazy.

I didn't understand how the Tyson I first met became the Tyson I was seeing now.

He was so charming, so romantic, so loving and now he was cold, distant, and manipulative.

I didn't know what to do.

As I lay in the bed beside my sleeping husband I resolved in my mind that I was not going to fall under Tyson's spell yet again.

I was not going to fall for his tactics any longer.

# Chapter Twelve

I was woken up out of my sleep due to feeling a weight on my head.

My eyes popped open and Tyson had his hand over my forehead.

He was trying to speak over me like some kind of voodoo or something. His eyes were closed, so he didn't realize I was awake.

He kept chanting some unintelligible words over me. He was repeating the same phrase over and over again.

I tried to get him to snap out of it.

"Tyson, what are you doing?" I sat up, which caused him to move back from his position of leaning over me with his hand on my forehead.

"You will never leave me," he said with venom in his tone.

"Did you just try to put a spell on me?"

"No. I was praying."

"That didn't sound like a prayer."

"How dare you judge me when I was just trying to keep us together. I was praying for us."

"Look, Tyson, I'm tired. Let's just go back to sleep."

We laid back down, but as I was drifting back off I heard Tyson chanting again under his breath.

———

The next day, the chant was bothering me, so I decided to talk to Tyson about it.

I went downstairs and expected to see him sitting in the living room, watching TV, but instead he was cooking breakfast, to my surprise.

I couldn't remember the last time Tyson lifted a finger in the kitchen.

He was slicing some apples with a butcher knife, so I started in.

"Tyson, last night when you were praying, or chanting, or whatever it was..."

He met my eyes. "What about it?"

"Why were you saying those things?"

He got that strange look in his eyes again.

"I received a special revelation from God."

My mind went blank.

"A revelation from God?"

He nodded.

"What kind of revelation?"

He chuckled.

"You wouldn't understand, Lexis."

"Tell me. Please." My eyes searched his.

He sighed. "I've been sent here from Heaven. I have a special gift where God tells me everything. You should appreciate that I chose to be your husband."

I didn't know what to say to that.

I was very confused.

Tyson continued. "The Lord revealed to me that we must stick together. I must be your pastor, and you must be my servant. I will reveal to you the hidden meanings of the scriptures as God reveals them to me. We start our first Bible study tonight."

I was speechless.

"So, you mean to tell me that I can't even go to my own church anymore?"

"I'm not saying that you can't, but what I am saying is that you need to be more dedicated to your household since I have decided to begin Bible studies for our family."

I held my peace.

---

A few weeks went by and Tyson really did begin the Bible study, but the odd thing was that although he was teaching the Bible, he wasn't even living by what he taught.

We had a nice night together, which was very rare these days.

We decided to watch a movie.

When Tyson went to the bathroom, his phone slipped out of his pocket without him realizing it when he got up from the couch.

I thought nothing of it, but then realized the phone was lighting up.

It was on silent, so I turned it over to look at the screen and saw a text message from a female name. I unlocked the phone and saw a series of messages between Tyson and some woman.

There were back and forth messages from that day, and then earlier messages dating back weeks, but all of his comments back to her seemed to be erased except the ones from today.

I snapped. I was not going to stand for this.

By the time Tyson returned from the bathroom the

movie was off and I was standing there with his phone in one hand and the other hand on my hip.

"You've been cheating on me?"

He looked bewildered.

"What are you talking about, Lexis?"

I showed him his phone screen, which was displaying the text messages. "This, Tyson. You and this other woman!"

"What are you doing with my phone?"

He grabbed it from me, not even looking at the screen as he returned it to his pocket.

"Tyson, how long have you been seeing this woman?"

"I'm not seeing any woman, Lexis. It's all in your mind."

"My mind didn't make up those text messages, Tyson."

"The girl had the wrong number. I was just being friendly."

"So how did the conversation go on for weeks?"

He switched the subject. "That was actually my homeboy's girlfriend. We were talking about my homeboy, not me."

I was not buying it this time.

"This is enough, Tyson. I want a divorce."

Tyson pleaded for me to forgive him.

"No."

I went upstairs and told him he could sleep in the living room.

He went to open the door to our bedroom, but I locked it.

I was walking toward the bed to prepare for sleep when Tyson spoke his next words.

"This house will be hell if you decide to leave me."

# Chapter THIRTEEN

The next day, Tyson was on his knees begging for my forgiveness.

I didn't want to hear it.

"Please, Lexis," he pleaded.

"No, Tyson. I have taken a lot of things during this marriage, but I can't take you cheating."

"Please. I have a friend who I trust. He does counseling. We can go to him. I promise I will give it a sincere try."

"No."

"Please, Lexis. Doesn't God hate divorce?"

He got me with that one.

Tyson knew that I loved the Lord with my whole heart.

Although I knew he was taking that scripture out of context, my mind went to Ja'el and Tamra, and all the people I knew. How was I going to explain a divorce?

I couldn't deal with the shame.

"Okay, Tyson. I will try the counseling."

―――

I had a conversation with Ja'el and Tamra later that week.

"Wow, Lexis. So glad to hear from you," Tamra said.

"Right, It's been ages," said Ja'el. "Ever since you married Tyson, you've been MIA."

"And what is that supposed to mean?" I snapped.

Tamra opened her mouth, but Ja'el cut in.

"It means that something is going on, but you're not telling us."

"What do you mean, something is going on? There is nothing going on with me!"

Tamra tried another approach. "We're just worried about you, Lexis."

"Worried? Worried for that? What is there to be worried about?"

Ja'el chimed in again. "Why are you so defensive if there aren't any problems? Are you and Tyson going through it? You can talk to us, Lexis."

"So, what you two are telling me is that you've been discussing me behind my back?"

Ja'el responded. "Not at all. We are simply two best friends who are wondering what's going on with their other best friend. That's all."

"We love you, Lexis," Tamra added.

Guilt filled my heart.

"Sorry, guys. I've just been so stressed with work."

*And life. And Tyson.*

"It's fine," Tamra said. "We just want you to know we're here for you."

---

We had the counseling session with Tyson's friend. Bryson was a well-respected colleague that Tyson had known for years.

We laid out our issues and Bryson sat there listening in silence.

When we finished, Bryson turned to Tyson.

"Brother, I feel like you need to learn how to deal with your wife better."

Tyson was immediately offended.

"Excuse me?"

Bryson tried to alleviate his concerns.

"I'm not saying you're a bad husband. I'm just saying that sometimes our communication styles can be improved."

"So, you think I don't know how to communicate? I am a very educated man, Bryson."

"I'm not saying that all, Brother. Sometimes people just hear and receive information in different ways, is all."

"So, you're saying I'm crazy."

"Tyson, I'm not saying any of those things."

"So why are you talking to me like I'm an idiot?"

Bryson tried to redirect.

"How about this? Before we come to the next session, Tyson, I want you to write down a list of the top five things you need from your wife. Lexis, I want you to do the same. How does that sound?"

Tyson calmed down.

"That sounds doable."

Bryson smiled.

"Great, man. See you next week."

As we got in the car, I thought we had broken new ground with this session, but Tyson quickly squelched that idea.

"That man has no idea what he is talking about. I will never go to him again!"

He stared at the building with a vengeful expression.

I didn't know what to do.

This was the one person Tyson claimed he trusted, yet he was turning his back on Bryson's advice as well.

If Tyson didn't listen to someone he had great respect for, who would he ever listen to?

# Chapter FOURTEEN

I was at my wits end.

I got home from work and decided to do some cleaning before Tyson came in.

As I was sweeping, I saw an earring in our bedroom that was not one of mine.

Tyson came home about an hour later.

I tried to find the best way to approach him.

As much as I thought about it, I found it was hard to find the words.

He ate his dinner, watched TV, and went on like he didn't have a care in the world.

Finally, I'd had enough.

When he came into our bedroom later on that night, I confronted him.

"Tyson, whose earring is this?"

He immediately became defensive. "I'm tired of you always insinuating things, Lexis. I don't know whose earring that is. It's probably yours."

I thought about my son who was in his room sleeping.

If he woke up and heard us yelling, it could hurt him.

I knew I had to calm down.

"We'll talk about this later."

Tyson wasn't backing down. "Lexis, it must be yours."

I refused to engage with him any further.

My mind was still on my son. This marriage was

starting to affect him. He was tired all the time from hearing Tyson and I arguing day after day.

---

I decided to give my son a break for the weekend.
He deserved some peace and to have some fun in the sun with his grandmother.

When my son was safely away, I decided to confront Tyson.

"Tyson, do you have a moment?"

He looked up from the TV. "What is it?"

"Remember the earring I saw?"

His expression darkened. "What about it?"

"If I can remember correctly, Tyson, the earring wasn't mine."

"Lexis, I don't know what you're talking about."

My mind was tired.

It wasn't worth the argument, going in circles over and over again, but ending with Tyson never admitting to what he did.

I pulled a sheet of paper from behind my back and held it before my husband.

"I want a divorce."

He looked surprised. "Divorce papers?"

I nodded.

His eyes widened as he jumped up from his seat. "You filed?"

He took a step toward me.

"No, but I was going to."

He got even closer. "Why would you do that?"

"It's not working out."

He took the paper and examined it.

I opened my mouth to say something else, but all of a sudden, Tyson put his hand on my mouth and pushed me onto the couch.

I couldn't breathe.

Tyson was so filled with rage he covered my nose and mouth with the paper and pinned me down as I fought for air.

I couldn't move, and Tyson was suffocating me with his body weight and the weight of the paper over my face.

I started screaming and trying to fight him off.

Finally, he snapped out of it and moved the paper from my face.

I gasped for air as I looked at my husband.

"Tyson, I was playing. I was playing."

My heart was gripped with fear.

He got off of me and I sat up.

"Now, what were you saying?" he asked.

"I was just playing. I was just joking, Tyson."

He stared at me.

"Stop being so serious. Come on, Tyson. Calm down."

He continued to stare for another moment before he returned to normal.

"If you are playing, then rip it up."

I immediately obeyed and smiled at him for good measure.

He was finally satisfied.

"Good. Now no more joking like that."

―――

After that incident, I realized that I had to do something soon.

I broke down and told Ja'el and Tamra what happened.

"I'm so sorry I didn't tell you guys sooner!" I wailed.

Tamra wrapped her arms around me, and Ja'el joined in the group hug.

Ja'el spoke up with tears in her eyes. "Lexis, we are going to help you develop a plan to get away from that man."

I was surprised to hear that, but grateful for my friends.

We talked all that afternoon, and by the time we finished, I felt like we had something concrete.

We had a plan.

I immediately put it into motion.

# Chapter FIFTEEN

I opened a bank account, had the cards sent to a PO box, and purchased a brand-new cell phone that I kept at my job.

I also started applying for apartments on my job computer.

I had to leave Tyson, and it needed to be a clean break because if I didn't someone was going to get hurt.

I started having part of the money from my paychecks routed to my new bank account so I could save up.

I was getting all my ducks in a row and I was trying my best to act normal at home.

———

At home, Tyson was getting bolder and bolder.

Now he was mowing the lawn with his shirt off and shooting flirty glances at the female neighbors.

They soaked it all up, but they barely said two words to me.

One day Tyson's sister came to visit us.

Tyson put on his usual charm, and it made me sick to my stomach.

When Tyson went to take a so-called business call, I took the opportunity to ask his sister a question.

"Do you all really believe the act your brother puts on?"

She looked confused. "Who, Tyson?"

My eyes narrowed. "Yes, Tyson. He acts completely different with me than he does with you guys."

"Lexis, I have no idea what you are talking about. You should stop being so paranoid."

"Please do not believe that your brother is actually treating me like a good husband is supposed to treat his wife."

I broke down crying and tried to tell his sister some of what Tyson had done to me.

I couldn't contain myself.

I was hoping Tyson's sister would console me, or at least provide more insight into her brother, but it was no use.

"Lexis, Tyson already told us what you are like. You need to calm down and stop accusing him of such things."

"He cheated on me! He's cheating right now. Can't you see?"

"You need to be grateful that you are married."

After that, Tyson returned to the room and he and his sister exchanged more small talk before she left.

I wanted to walk right out the door behind her.

―――

The next day at work, I was reflecting about all that was going on and started having a panic attack.

I couldn't control my breathing. I was overcome with emotion.

My boss walked by and popped her head in my office.

"Hey. Lexis, what's going on?"

Her face was etched with concern.

I didn't want to tell her what I was going through.

It was way too painful and humiliating.

On one side, Tyson's friends and family thought I was crazy, and on the other, all of my friends and family would probably say they told me so.

How would I ever live this down?

How would I ever recover from this bad decision?

Right when I was considering changing my mind, my son's face flashed through my mind.

He didn't deserve this.

I needed to go through with my plan.

# Chapter SIXTEEN

One night, I was sleeping and woke up to see Tyson's side of the bed empty.

I heard voices coming from downstairs, so I crept down and caught Tyson red-handed video chatting with another woman.

What made matters worse was the woman was one of his friend's wives.

Tyson hung up as soon as he saw me standing there.

I crossed my arms.

"What are you going to tell me now, Tyson? Another wrong number?"

"You don't know what you are talking about."

"Yes, I do Tyson. You were just sitting here on a video chat with her!"

"Okay!" he yelled, startling me. "Yes, I was talking to another woman."

I burst into tears.

"Lexis," he tried to console me.

He wrapped me up in a hug, but I felt nothing but contempt toward him.

"How do you think that it's okay for a man to talk to another woman when his wife is sleeping upstairs?"

His expression turned cold.

"You should be happy you have a husband at all."

I broke down and started crying again.

He just looked at me like I was doing something wrong.

"Every woman wants to be married, but you just don't appreciate your marriage."

I ran upstairs to our bedroom.

Tyson didn't follow me.

―――

The next day, Ja'el and Tamra called me on three way.

"Are we still on for the plan?" Tamra asked. "We got your back. We are going to help you out. We just want to know if you're really ready for this?"

I hesitated. "No, I'm really not ready. I know I have to do it, but I'm not ready emotionally. I still love this man."

Ja'el tried to reassure me. "Lexis, you have to do it. It's the best thing for you and your child."

"I don't know, guys."

Tamra cut in. "Lexis, think about your son. I don't mean to keep bringing him up, but you know he is seeing how Tyson is treating you, right?"

She got me with that one.

"You don't deserve this, Lexis," Ja'el added. "No woman does."

I finally gave in.

"Okay. I'm going through with the plan."

I knew that with God all things were possible.

I just have to ask Him to bring me through.

"Lord," I prayed. "Give me strength."

―――

I continued my home life as I had been doing, cooking, cleaning, and catering to my son and Tyson.

Tyson didn't seem to suspect anything.

He was so busy with his outside life. It was likely he wouldn't notice anything, anyway.

When I was at work, I continued saving money and developing the plan.

# Chapter SEVENTEEN

The next day, I went to work and saw a missed call from the apartment complex on my other cell phone.

I called the number back and the landlord said I could move in.

I had saved enough for the first and last month's rent, which was all they were asking for.

I could pick up the keys today.

On my lunch break I raced over to the complex to meet with the landlord.

She was a really nice lady.

I paid her the money and looked around the apartment.

It was nice and spacious with plenty of room for me and my son.

I couldn't wait for it to be my home.

The only thing left was to move in, but I found myself crippled with fear.

At the same time, I was happy to know that there was a new beginning waiting for me.

*But if Tyson finds out, he will kill me! I know it.*

I swallowed my fears.

I knew life would be better on the other side.

―――

When I got home from work, Tyson was watching TV.

I cooked and cleaned, and he got in the shower.

When he came back downstairs, I asked him what he was doing.

"I'm going out with my boys."

Of course, a few hours later, Tyson sent a text saying that he had too much to drink so he was staying the night with his friend.

I knew full well that he was lying because it was barely eight o'clock, but I didn't fight him.

*Okay.*

Then I called Tamra and Ja'el.

It just so happened that both of them were free that evening.

"Can you guys help me move?"

"When?" they asked in unison.

"Right now."

"We're on our way," Ja'el said.

———

Before I knew it, all of me and my son's belongings were packed into a U-Haul.

I took one last look at the house.

It was two o'clock in the morning.

I hadn't heard from Tyson since he said he was staying the night with his friend.

I placed my wedding ring and key to Tyson's house on the counter, along with signed copies of the divorce papers.

"Goodbye," I said and walked out the door to my new life.

# Chapter EIGHTEEN

I hope you enjoyed reading Lexis' story, but what I say next may be shocking for some readers. Although Lexis and Tyson are fictional characters, their experiences were based on a true story.

I was a woman who was married to a narcissist. He lied to me and manipulated me, and his actions made me feel as if I were going crazy.

I developed a plan much like what Lexis did, and I was able to safely get away.

How did I develop my plan you might ask?

I had help from some good friends, family, and the Lord.

Not only did I have to develop a plan to get out of the dangerous situation I was in, I also had to stick to it. Because of my former husband's effect on my mind, I wrestled back and forth with thoughts of whether I should stay or go.

But just like Lexis, I thought of my future as well as my loved ones, and I knew I had to make a change. So, I did. I figured out what steps I needed to take, prayed to God for strength, and put the plan into motion.

It took me a while to get everything in place, but the reward of being free and having peace was worth it.

When I left my ex-husband, one of the main things I battled with was the idea of going back to him. Of course, he called and texted me many times, begging to know where I was staying, and asking if I could come visit him to rekindle.

I had to make up in my mind to refuse his advances. Despite what he said to get me to come back, I knew it would be short lasting. If I decided to give him another chance, since he never truly saw the error of his ways, he would go right back to the way he had been treating me, and likely become even worse.

Sometimes we can get free, but we also have to remain free. That's the part that takes the most work.

# Chapter NINETEEN

I want to take this time to outline some signs that you are dealing with a narcissist, as well as demonstrate the dangers of remaining in a relationship or marriage with one.

The first thing we should probably do is define exactly what a narcissist is. According to mental health experts, a narcissist is someone who has an overinflated sense of self-importance, or who is overly obsessed with his or her successes (https://www.verywellmind.com).

Some of the signs of a narcissist are: having a grandiose attitude; exaggerating one's importance; exaggerating abilities, accomplishments, or talents; craving admiration and acknowledgement; being preoccupied with power; having an exaggerated sense of uniqueness; having an entitled mentality; exploiting others for personal gain; and lacking in empathy (https://www.verywellmind.com).

This list is not all-inclusive, but it does give a good idea of what narcissists are like.

In the story, we can easily see that Tyson displayed almost all of these traits. At one point he told Lexis that he believed he had received special insight or revelation from God. At other points, he constantly reminded her that he didn't feel she was serving him enough, or meeting his needs despite the fact that she was doing the majority of the work for their household. Lastly, Tyson often had an entitled attitude, forcing Lexis to give up things that were important to her to please him.

Now that we've seen the signs, what are the dangers of staying with a narcissist?

In the story, we see that Tyson started off with just a narcissistic attitude, but after a while he segued into physical abuse. He threatened Lexis with his words, body language, and actions. He got to the point where he told her he would kill her if she left him. If someone is threatening to kill you then you need to develop a plan to leave him or her. Thankfully, Lexis was able to get away, but if she had stayed, Tyson would have likely fulfilled his promise to do her harm.

One final note: You cannot gain closure with a narcissist because the overwhelming majority of the time, they cannot and will not change. If you are in a serious relationship with a narcissist that is damaging your health or emotional wellbeing the best option for you is to leave the situation.

# Chapter TWENTY

As I previously mentioned, I was married to a narcissist.

I went through a great deal of mental anguish for the duration of our marriage because my ex-husband kept doing things very similar to what Tyson did to Lexis, but he would always cover it up by making it seem like I was imagining it all, or that I had made it up and accused him of something he wasn't doing.

This is called gaslighting, and it wreaked havoc on my mind for a long time.

After I left my ex-husband, I had to go through years of healing. I stayed in prayer and studying my Bible. I had to learn to love myself all over again.

I loved myself enough to leave my ex-husband in the first place, and to stay gone, ignoring his advances, but I had to relearn me.

I had to realize that there was nothing wrong with me.

I was a woman who was looking for love and I happened to find the opposite of what I prayed for. It wasn't my fault that my ex-husband was the way he was, and I did not deserve his treatment.

God brought me out of my trial and I was able to break free from the thoughts of unworthiness, embarrassment, shame, and humiliation that once held me in bondage.

If you are or have been in a relationship or marriage

with a narcissist, you too can be free. It will take time, effort, tears, and a plan, but with God, all things are possible.

Before I end this book, I want to leave you with some steps to emotional healing that helped me. I believe they will help you too:

1. Accept what went wrong in the relationship
2. Accept the part you played in the demise of the relationship
3. Don't blame yourself for the other person's actions
4. Forgive yourself and forgive the other person
5. Meditate on Scriptures related to healing (Mark 12:31, Matthew 22:36-40)
6. Study Scriptures on love (Psalm 147:3, John 14:27)
7. PRAY and ask God for healing
8. Seek counsel if you need to

**These things will help to bring you to a place of wholeness. Remember, healing after a broken relationship can be difficult and emotional, but with God, all things are possible (Matthew 19:26).**

**Embrace the possibilities that come along with a fresh start in life.**

Minister Janell Brown

www.ingramcontent.com/pod-product-compliance
Lightning Source LLC
Chambersburg PA
CBHW070949180426
43194CB00041B/1957